Memoir of a Chubby Child

Memoir of a Chubby Child

My Truth About Growing Up Fat

Jean M. Jerome

Surrogate Press®

Copyright ©2020 Jean M. Jerome
All rights reserved.
No part of this publication may be reproduced, stored in a retrieval system, or transmitted in any form or by any means, electronic, mechanical, photocopying, recording, or otherwise, without written permission of the author.

Published in the United States by
Surrogate Press®
an imprint of Faceted Press®
Surrogate Press, LLC
Park City, Utah
SurrogatePress.com

ISBN: 978-1-947459-45-8
Library of Congress Control Number: 2020918377

Book Cover and Interior design by:
Katie Mullaly, Surrogate Press®

To all the "chubby" girls out there, there is so much more to your life than your dress size.

Trust me, I know.

Table of Contents

Introduction 1

Chapter 1: The Sinful Nun 3

Chapter 2: The "It's Just Baby Fat" Myth 8

Chapter 3: The Electric Metronome 13

Chapter 4: The Girl Scout Blues 23

Chapter 5: As a Fat Girl, Am I Worthy of Love? 34

Chapter 6: Tell Someone Who Cares! 39

Chapter 7: My Year in Purgatory 59

Chapter 8: Where Would You Like It, Sir? 80

Chapter 9: Family Foibles 92

Chapter 10: The .05% Factor 97

Chapter 11: The Chubby Girl's Abbreviated
Guide for Fashion and Dieting 106

Chapter 12: A List of Synonyms for the
Word "Chubby" 107

Acknowledgments 109

About the Author 110

Introduction

Reflecting back on my life, I must admit that much of the stresses and anxieties that I faced were complicated by my own perceptions about my weight. Indeed, for most of my life I've fought with my weight, and I've never really won the battle. I have weighed as much as 283 pounds and as little as 132 pounds. I've been on a myriad of diets and lost and regained literally hundreds of pounds.

Now, as an extremely mature woman, I can look back and realize that despite the weight rollercoaster that I rode for so many years, I've had a pretty great life! I've finally learned that I have been my own worst enemy! Most of my battles revolved around my own insecurities. And, in retrospect, I realize that most of those doubts were definitely self-inflicted!

The world at large has always found me to be pleasant, bright, charming, and yes, attractive! I never lacked for suitors, and when I found the right guy for me, we got married; that was 49 years ago. I had a long career in education, and my weight was never an issue to anyone, except to me.

Since I've retired, I've decided to try my hand at writing, an avocation I'd always wanted to pursue. I've written a collection of short stories, mostly from my youth. These are real events that involve me and those around me. The stories are a peek into my life as a chubby, young girl. They are both a reflection about how my size affected me, and it's also snippets from a young girl's life and how she perceived what others thought of her! I hope you'll find them amusing; they really are all true stories!

The Sinful Nun
Chapter 1

"This is going to be a wonderful day," I thought. "I can't believe it! I am the Queen of the Holy Ascension Day Parade!" Saint Paul's held an annual parade to celebrate Mary's Ascension into Heaven. The parochial students from the parish were the main feature in the pageantry that was to begin in the church parking lot and end up inside the church. The parents were beginning to arrive and the lot quickly filled. Cameras with big lenses sparkled in the afternoon sun. According to my teacher Sister Mary Magdalena, this was a "Sacred Event" in tribute to the Virgin Mary's holy and virginal life style.

As a third grader, I was overwhelmed by the mysteries and rituals of the Catholic Church. However, if Sister Mary Magdalena said it was a "Sacred Event," that was good enough for me. And I was the Queen! I calculated that the nuns selected me because I was the holiest, most pure student. I figured I was probably the girl who most closely resembled the Virgin Mary. As I grew older I realized that the reason I had been chosen was probably because I was the largest third grade girl and most able to carry the heavy Virgin Mary's Flag as I led the parade. It really didn't matter why I was selected. All I knew for sure was that I got to wear a pretty dress, while the rest of the students were relegated to their school uniforms: navy blue blazers; gaberdine, navy blue jumpers; and gray knee socks.

I wore a light beige, taffeta dress with a chocolate brown, velvet Peter Pan collar and sash. Lacy, white anklets and patent leather Mary Jane's accented my ensemble. Because I was a chubby, short girl, my mother didn't normally dress me in starched crinoline petticoats. However, because this was a "Sacred Event" I was allowed to wear two of them. My dress ballooned and billowed around me; the petticoats were uncomfortable and really scratched. I looked like Tweedle Dum with a case of hives, but I didn't care; I felt beautiful and very holy!

My mother had paid particular attention to my hair. Most days I wore long pigtails that my mother dutifully braided each morning. Since this was a "Sacred Event," my mother had only partially braided the hair, curled the bottoms into sausage curls and securely fastened the curls across the back of my head with hair pins and clips. When she finished, I looked into the mirror and saw cascading curls down my back! I was sure that the Virgin Mary would think I was beautiful and worthy.

At any rate, the other nuns worked with Sister Mary Magdalena to line up the different classes for the parade. As Queen, I stood at the head of the line. While waiting in line, I vigorously started to scratch my inner left thigh. The petticoats were merciless. As I stood scratching my thigh, I was viciously smacked on the back of the head. My hairpins and hair clips flew in all directions, and my curls quickly wilted! I reeled around and stared up into Sister Mary Magdalena's beet-red face. Sister snarled, "I know what you are doing, young lady, and you will go to Hell for it!"

I was stunned; I actually stopped breathing! I had absolutely no idea what Sister Mary Magdalena was talking about. I stammered, "My petticoats are scratching me." Sister Mary Magdalena delivered a second mighty blow that sent me staggering and she screamed, "Don't you dare lie to me. The Virgin Mary knows that you are lying!" I froze; I just stood there as tears rolled down my cheeks. Sister Angelica scurried to my side to help quell Sister Mary Magdalena's rage. All the students were staring and giggling. "Queenie" was in big trouble!

Sister Angelica stammered, "We'll discuss this after the service, Sister Mary Magdalena. Now it's time to begin the procession." And so, with a tear-stained, down-turned face and drooping curls askew, I picked up the heavy Virgin Mary's sacred flag and slowly headed towards the church entrance, with the procession following me.

The day was ruined. My mother's questioning stare followed me down the center aisle. I should have felt holy and radiant, but instead I feared the Virgin Mary might actually descend, point her finger at me and whisper, "Sinner!" When I passed my father, he lowered his camera and took no pictures. I silently lamented, *"Oh, No! Everyone knows I am going straight to Hell! But, what did I do?"*

After the ceremony, I crawled into the back seat of the family car and remained mute on the way home. My mother had prepared my favorite meal, breaded pork chops with mashed potatoes. Normally I would have been an animated chatterbox. However, on that day I silently pushed the food around on my plate. Not even my mother's German chocolate cake, usually my favorite, got me talking!

I refused to speak to anyone about Sister Mary Magdalena's anger, but the memory of that day continued to haunt me for many years. In fact, I didn't figure it out until I was 22 years old! This is what Sister Mary Magdelena thought I'd been doing on that fateful day.

It was a lazy summer afternoon as I sat in a comfy armchair engrossed in a newly-released, steamy best seller touted as a "torrid romance novel," it unexpectedly struck me! I dropped the novel into my lap and moaned, "Oh No! That's what Sister Mary Magdalena was thinking! That's awful; how could she?"

As I reflected on this purely Catholic phenomenon, I realized that I might, indeed, be doomed to Hell. But if masturbation really was a reason for eternal damnation, then I knew that I would be in the presence of good company: friends, neighbors, relatives, loved ones, kings, queens, movie stars, lawyers, priests, doctors, teachers, and, of course politicians, to name a few! Perhaps I might even meet up again with Sister Mary Magdalena!

The "It's Just Baby Fat" Myth
Chapter 2

As you already know, I was a pampered, spoiled, but adorable child! I had never anguished over my perpetual chubbiness. My mother had repeatedly told me not to concern myself about my weight problem. "It's just baby fat," she assured me! And... stupidly, I believed her! Certainly my mother wouldn't fib!

It was not until I reached puberty that I realized my mother was a blatant liar! And now, as a pre-teenager, my weight had ballooned to almost 225 pounds, plus, I was "becoming a woman!" **UGH!** It was not a happy time in my life! I vowed to go on a diet; however, I had certainly no idea about how one would diet. My mother was certainly no help! She weighed well over 300 pounds and, to me, she seemed content. Spoiler Alert: she was not!

My fellow friends were discovering boys, and they seemed to know how to behave around the opposite sex. I, on the other hand, became the neighborhood tomboy. The boys all liked me and joked with me, but just not in "that way!" I had no idea how to flirt. Besides, who would want to flirt with a beached whale!

And so, I spent way too many lonely weekends eating potato chips, munching on M&Ms, and slurping down sugary sodas with my fellow "loser" buddies! Meanwhile, it seemed, all the pretty girls had boyfriends and wore their guys' class rings, tightly wrapped in pastel angora yarn, which they constantly combed to fluff up their prized rings! The cool girls clung to their boyfriends and wore their jocks' varsity jackets, while the losers dragged out *Ouija Boards* and *Crazy Eight Balls* to predict hopeful boyfriends in the future. Despite our optimistic natures, the Talking Board usually pointed to a lonely, solitary life!

I would faithfully begin a diet each Monday morning. However, by noon I was already famished and devoured a calorie–laden lunch. I rationalized that I had already blown my diet for the week and vowed I would start anew on the following Monday. That "Circle of Life" routine became a new norm for me! Weight loss... **NADA!** Remaining obese became a justification badge of honor for me, and I was able to explain away my lack of suitors by simply saying silly things like, "Who wants a boyfriend, anyway?" or "If only I wasn't so fat, I'd have plenty of boyfriends!"

My mom demanded that I sign up for a co-ed ballroom dance class through Parks & Recreation. There I learned, among other dances, the Cha-Cha and the Waltz. There was a culminating event at the end of the season. Suits for the boys and fancy dresses for the girls were required, and everybody had to wear white gloves. It was to be a "fancy-schmancy" occasion!

In the late fifties there were no stores that catered to overweight teens. After days of searching, my mother found a solitary dress that would fit me. It was an off-white, stiffly brocaded sheath at *Lane Bryant's*, a grandmother's party dress. It was meant for a dowager and was truly hideous, but at least I wouldn't pop a button or break a zipper. I hoped the white gloves would detract from the dress! As expected on that fateful night, I remained the last girl to be asked to glide onto the dance floor and dazzle everyone with my Cha-Cha-Cha! Who really cared? **ME!**

I remained overweight throughout my sophomore year in high school. I had many friends and had developed a keen sense of dark humor. I seemed to enjoy making fun of myself, and those close to me found me to be hilarious! I belonged to many clubs. Heck... I was even the president of the German Club...**WUNDERBAR!**

The fall of my sophomore year, I began to allow myself to rethink about how my life might change if I actually lost weight. My obsession with the teen idol Fabian had peaked, and I imagined he would take me into his arms and *Turn Me Loose!* However, that remained a fantasy!

I had a crush on my long-time neighbor. Tom was actually a year younger than I, but seemed quite mature, and he was well built and always smelled wonderful; I believe it was *English Leather*. We had been close friends for years and he usually came over to our house at least once a day. He would put his arm around me as we sat in our den and listened to various show tunes and comedy albums on the record player. We both loved *West Side Story* and the *Smothers Brothers*. Sadly, Tom had a real girlfriend, a neighbor; Alice, lived next door. She was slender, chic, and aloof; I was chubby, adoring and eager to please. Alas, my crush was also crushed. Alice won!

Still, I began to start watching what I put into my mouth and I actually began to lose some weight. And then, life forever changed... On November 22nd,

1963, the principal's somber voice came over the loudspeaker as I sat in my afternoon German class. John F. Kennedy had been shot and killed in Dallas, Texas. I remember that my German teacher fell sobbing to the floor. She had been a prisoner of war during World War II and she escaped with her family and made it to America. She couldn't believe that such a horrific deed could happen here.

All our lives changed on that day! Dieting became a non-issue. America stumbled through the next few months, but slowly the healing process began as the world began to look for guidance with Lyndon B Johnson at the helm. He was not a smooth talker like JFK. Johnson was deliberate; he had a domineering personality.

Meanwhile, my munching escalated again. Soon I had regained those lost pounds! I did have one date to a formal dance that spring. He was Mormon, and can you believe it… he had never drunk a Coca Cola! As you can well imagine, we were not headed for any romantic entanglements!

I finally shed those unwanted pounds during my senior year. However, I need to refer you to a future story, "My Year in Purgatory," to learn more about my seemingly endless journey to weight loss!

The Electric Metronome
Chapter 3

My father was hopeful that at least one of his three children would become a musical prodigy. As a young adult he aspired to become a concert violinist. However, when he married my mother in 1928 there was not a huge demand for concert violinists. A practical man, he refocused his many talents and eventually became a prominent aeronautical engineer; but in the early days he subsidized his salary by teaching violin to, as he always put it, "tone-deaf, snot-nosed children." As an engineer, he became well known throughout the nation for his accomplishments in the era of the burgeoning Space Age. My father still remained faithful to the study of classical violin as an avocation. As his engineering career spiraled and we relocated to new states, he continued to perform as the First Chair Violinist in several city philharmonics, and he practiced for hours each night.

As the youngest child, I became my father's last hope for a musical prodigy in the family. Though both my older brother and sister fared well at piano, according to my father, they lacked the necessary zeal to pursue the violin. So, at the tender age of six, I was handed my first violin. My father had actually hired a violin artisan to craft a child-size violin scaled to match my small stature. Up to this point in my life, I had been a carefree, happy-go-lucky, mischievous, but adorable, chubby child. The fact that I could have cared less about the violin always frustrated and angered my dad. Fortunately for me, he couldn't break my spirit. I would giggle my way through *Twinkle, Twinkle Little Star*. I dragged my bow across the strings in a halting and screeching fashion.

As I recall, one night my father collapsed into the recliner, and screamed to my mother who was washing dinner dishes. He growled, "This one will never be a violinist!" He grabbed the customized case, threw the small violin into it and tossed the case into the hall closet. With a scowl, he looked at me and sternly said, "You will begin your piano lessons next week!" I was relieved. Little did I know that I was jumping from the frying pan into the fire!

I studied piano from age six until I was 21 years old. I do not recall any fond memories! Technically speaking, I was quite strong; what I lacked was passion, zeal, and diligence. I did not have the soul of a pianist, but my big sister did. She would plunk her rather large derrière down onto the piano bench, and with a dramatic flourish and a soulful gaze, she would bend over the keyboard and sway with the music as she played. Depending on the musical selection, she could appear sad or serene, agitated or whimsical. Often she would close her eyes as she played and swayed. I thought she was a big ham!

I, on the other hand, would plunk down with a loud thud and instantly begin pounding the keys as my fingers raced across the keyboard. I simply wanted to get through it! I only played in ***crescendo***; no ***pianissimo*** tones were ever heard from me. The music would continue to get louder and faster, and I always finished in ***forte*** with a loud, miss-struck, dissonant chord.

I could not keep time. I had only one tempo... high-speed! My father would stand behind me and try to keep me on tempo by waving a conductor's wand at me and counting out each measure. He would keep this up until I started to cry and then he would retreat and stomp into his study. I might add that these were **daily** practice sessions. Following the daily torture, I would drag myself into the kitchen where my dear mother always had a plate full of cookies and a glass of milk waiting for me. Of course, this contributed to my burgeoning weight problem, but at that moment in time, it was always comforting.

On my ninth birthday my father handed me a beautifully wrapped package. He could barely contain his excitement. I tore through the wrapping paper, opened the lid and peered into the box; I had no idea what it was. Father lifted the apparatus from the box and proudly exclaimed, "It's an electric metronome!"

He plugged it in, set the dial and placed it on top of the piano. It provided a rhythmic beat and flashing red light to help set the pianist's tempo. What a great gift for a nine year old! Unfortunately, the metronome really didn't help me. I would either stare too long at the red, pulsating light and lose my place, or I was lulled into a hypnotic stupor and just sat there with my hands hovering above the keys.

I took private lessons from a nun at the local Catholic women's college. I always dreaded those weekly lessons. I knew it must have cost my parents lots of money to send me to Sister Thoma. My mother had never learned how to drive, so she would send me by taxi to the college located at the city's east border. I always wore a frown and had an upset stomach on the way to my lesson. The return trip was much more cheerful; I was free for another week!

Sister Thoma was stern and demanding. She also held a conductor's wand that she would freely use to rap me on the knuckles if I didn't raise my fingers high enough above the keys. Every lesson started with drills: scales, chords and *arpeggios*. These exercises were taken from the **Czerny Finger Exercises** book. I loathed them and seldom practiced them at home; so each week I received a repetitive lecture on the merits of **Czerny's** book.

Next, we would move on to whatever the current musical selection Sister Thoma had selected for me. My favorite composer was Beethoven; most of his works were loud and heavy. Bach required considerable dexterity in the left hand because the left hand would have to echo the melody from the right hand. Mozart was also a good choice, but I disliked Chopin; he created too many waltzes! Of course every young lady pianist could play *Clair de Lune* and *Rhapsody in Blue*. I was never allowed to play any contemporary music; there would be no show tunes for me. The one and only piece of contemporary music that I was allowed to play was called *Sputnik Boogie*; it was a product of the times. Each lesson would end with ten minutes of sight-reading; I loathed this part of the lesson. By now I was tired and Sister Thoma had lost all patience. Every lesson ended on a sour note.

I hated to perform for an audience, but Sister Thoma required it. There were usually three recitals a year. I have blocked most of those miserable memories from my mind. I do remember playing the piano on stage and staring at Sister Thoma standing behind the curtains. Her face was contorted and beet red. Simultaneously, out of the corner of my right eye, I could see my father slink down in his seat. I had inadvertently switched composers half way through the selection. The *First Movement* was a Beethoven Sonata; somehow I transitioned into a Mozart Sonata in the *Second Movement*. It was a smooth transition; no one else noticed. My father and Sister Thoma, however, were not amused.

I was never in control at the piano; it controlled me! I would watch my fingers as I played and really had no idea what I was playing. I continuously pumped the foot pedals; I had no idea why. When I was a sophomore in high school Sister Thoma entered me into a competition. The winner would receive a free month at the famed Michigan Interlochen Summer Music Camp. I was required to memorize nine musical selections plus perform the dreaded scales. chords and *arpeggios*. My father was very excited about the prospect of his daughter being accepted into this famous camp. He drilled me for weeks. My mother calmly said, "What will be, will be."

Five judges were seated in the balcony that day. I was actually going through the motions with few hesitations. I had only one more selection to perform, the *Donkey Serenade*. I loved that piece, but on Page Two I faltered and stopped. The head judge flew down the balcony stairs waving the sheet music at me. As she neared me, she actually said, "My Dear, you play beautifully. We will allow you to look at the music; please just finish the piece. "I took the sheet music from her and stared down at the notes. I had absolutely no idea what they meant or where to place my fingers. That morning I actually learned the true meaning of the expression, "My mind went blank." I stared at the hieroglyphics on the sheet for a long time, handed the music back to her and said, "I'm sorry, I can't read the notes." In spite of this, I still took 2nd Place. I was good, but I was just not good enough for Interlochen. I thought, "Well, what was, was!"

Summers were always my favorite time of year. My parents owned a great summer home on a beautiful lake in Michigan. I was free in the summer because there was no piano there. The days were filled with swimming, sailing, waterskiing, walking and reading. Sadly, the summer of my sophomore year in high school my father bought me another surprise.

My mother, sister and I had gone to an afternoon matinee. I was anxious to get home and jump into the lake to cool off. My father greeted us at the back door; he was beaming! I walked into the living room and there it stood against the front wall; dad had bought me a brand new upright piano. It was even equipped with an electric heater to protect it from dampness and keep the keys in tune. My summer freedom quickly slipped away; I now had to practice at least one hour per day and resume my piano lessons. I would sit and stare out at the lake as I pounded the keys. I definitely mastered the "soulful gaze" that summer!

Because of my father's career, we reluctantly moved to Southern California the summer of 1964 after my junior year in high school I would be attending a new school for my senior year! Of course, I was beyond depressed, but I figured that at least my piano days were over. WRONG! My dad researched and found a private piano teacher for me. She was a very old, Swedish woman, and she always wore a high-necked, long, black dress, and she regularly stuffed a white lace handkerchief into her right cuff. Mrs. Volemy always stood at my right side and, with fingers shaking, she would often grab my shoulder. In retrospect, I think she did this to help maintain her balance. However, at that time, I always thought I had made a mistake and I'd blurt out, "OOPS!" After I had blurted that phrase multiple times, she told me to stop playing. She aimed a bony, shriveled finger at me and whispered, "If you must say anything, say 'Excuse me!" I must have said, "Excuse me" a thousand times during my senior year, but at least she was still alive when I graduated!

I continued with piano at the university. My father paid extra tuition so that I could study with the head professor. He did not care for me because I was not a music major. I rarely practiced until the day before my lesson. I often took my latest boyfriend to the reserved practice room. It was a quiet place to make out.

The last musical composition that I attempted was a melancholy piece called *Autumn Leaves*. As always, I played it in high gear. I remember my professor saying to me, "My Dear, slow down! It is not a bloody hurricane; the leaves are gently falling!" That was the last semester that I studied piano at the university. It seemed the professor's schedule was completely full, and he now only accepted music majors.

It has taken me well over fifty years to recapture any desire to play a piano. I would like to be able to sit down and select any piece of music I wanted to play and then just play it the way I wanted to play it. It might be too loud or off-tempo, but it would be a wonderful form of self-expression. With that kind of thinking, however, I will never see the Summer Music Camp at Interlochen.

The Girl Scout Blues
Chapter 4

Scouting really wasn't as great as everyone had told me it would be. Mom and dad had explained that it would be a super way to make new friends, to participate in many fun activities, including camp, and to build good character. My parents thought it would be an excellent opportunity for me to become involved in our new neighborhood. "*Whatever*," I dismally thought to myself!

On a family vote of 2 to 1, mom enrolled me into the neighborhood Brownie Troop #7. Mom had trouble locating a Brownie uniform large enough to fit me. I was sturdy, short, and definitely overweight.

Looking at my reflection in the mirror, I saw a chubby girl in an ugly brown dress with gaping button holes across my belly. Plus, the brown beanie atop my braids did little to enhance my appearance. I was pretty sure Brownies was not going to be lots of fun, despite my parents' cheerful endorsements.

And so, with a pout, drooping shoulders, and considerable apprehension, I was shuttled to my first meeting. The leader was a scrawny, pale but cheerful woman with big teeth and a bigger hairdo! Mrs. Gray wore a perpetual smile across her face. Her teased, dishwater blond hair formed a large halo around her surprisingly sharp, bird-like features. She was dressed in a Brownie sweatshirt, jeans and sneakers. She spoke in questions:

- "Are we the best Brownie troop ever?"
- "Are we going to have lots of fun?"
- "Shall we sing another Brownie tune?"
- "Ladies, are we going to quiet down, sit up straight and pay attention?"
- "Do we need to take a potty break?"

A cynic at Grade 4, I thought, *"I don't know about you, Mrs. Gray, but I gotta take a pee!"*

By contrast, Mrs. Swank, the co-leader, was a sultry brunette. She was an aging beauty who wore pounds of makeup and scarlet red lipstick, lots of hairspray, and way too much perfume; she really reeked! She was dressed in tight, black spandex-like pedal pushers, a hugging V-necked bright, stark yellow tee shirt that revealed her ample bosom, and strappy, black sandals. Her neon-colored nails and toes, coupled with enormous gold hoop earrings, completed "The Look."

Mrs. Swank was always very quiet and often rolled her eyes and yawned. She really seemed bored with the Brownies. However, she came alive during the singing portion of the meetings. It was rumored that Mrs. Swank had once been a Las Vegas starlet.

I scanned my fellow Brownies. They were all tiny, blond, and petite with blue eyes and large dimples. A few wore braces and one girl wore thick glasses, but even they were very cute.

I quickly observed that I was definitely the fattest Brownie and probably the least pretty. It depressed me and made me want to eat. I couldn't wait until treats would be served! In fact, eating became my favorite Brownie pastime!

Well, the singing wasn't too bad. In a falsetto, Mrs. Swank would lead us in the favorite Brownie classics: *"Make New Friends And Keep The Old," I Have Something In My Pocket That Belongs Across My Face," "99 Bottles Of Beer On The Wall."* and the ever-favorite *"Cowboy Petie, Bloody And Dead."* I definitely enjoyed the singing; I didn't sing well, but I could sing loudly!

The only other activity that worked for me was Origami, Japanese paper folding. Although no one could ever clearly identify my creations, I didn't have to exert much energy to fold paper, and I mastered the skill of eating cookies as I folded paper into questionable shapes. Oh well, maybe Girl Scouts would be better... It wasn't!

In 5th grade, I was promoted or passed on to the Girl Scouts. My new leader was a mousy woman who never raised her voice or smiled. Mrs. Stickler always wore a sad face. If the truth be told, I didn't think much of Mrs. Stickler. The meetings were BORING and the treats were unimaginative and way too healthy! I longed for the potato chips, dips, and cokes that Mrs. Swank had provided. In a low monotone, Mrs. Stickler would drone on about badges to be earned, community service to be performed, and she also provided occasional good dental hygiene tips. The meetings were as drab as Mrs. Stickler's wardrobe.

I did love my new green Girl Scout uniform, and the matching green beret provided a French flair! I loved the darker green sash that was worn diagonally across my chest. I hadn't earned any badges yet, but the sash did hide the gaping buttons problem across my belly! I decided the sash was slimming and took to wearing it on top of every outfit.

Fortunately for me, Mrs. Stickler was replaced mid-year. Tragically, it seems she had suffered a nervous breakdown. Mrs. Jones, Mrs. Stickler's replacement, was young, beautiful and downright perky! Though I normally didn't lean towards "perky," Mrs. Jones was very cool; she even allowed us to call her by her first name. Lucy Jones knew how

The Girl Scout Blues

to have fun, and she served great treats! *"Maybe Girl Scouts really is going to be fun,"* I reflected. Unfortunately, the dream quickly took on a nightmarish tone!

My first humiliating experience occurred in April of my 5th grade year. The troop members were collectively working on performing arts badges. Lucy Jone's Girl Scout Troop #17 was entered into a regional Girl Scout talent show. Everyone in the troop, except me, was very excited about the upcoming event.

Troop #17 would perform an authentic, Hawaiian hula dance on stage!

If that wasn't bad enough, the mother volunteers decided to make crepe paper hula skirts and tops for the entire troop! The girls were to be measured at the next meeting. *"Oh, No!"* I panicked. *"I don't want to be measured!"*

On that fateful day, I repeatedly retreated to the back of the line; I was the last scout to be measured. One mother threw the tape measure around me and loudly announced the numbers to a second mother to record. The other girls had tiny measurements; on the average, the measuring mother announced: Bust–28"...Waist–22"...Hips–26". And then there was me: Bust–40"...Waist–33"... Hips–38". Everyone abruptly stopped talking! The mothers collectively thought, "Is she really that big? Will we have to buy more crepe paper?" I wanted to die! I was the only girl in 5th grade with a bosom. I had already outgrown my training bra. The thought of a wispy crepe paper top was terrifying. I pondered, *"There must be a shortage of coconut shells!"*

I did survive that awful afternoon, but now I began to fret about the pending talent show. Mercifully, Lucy Jones reassigned me from "Hula Dancer" to "Hula Announcer." I was sure it was because Lucy didn't want a gyrating hippo messing up the authentic hula number, but I was grateful. I simply had to stand at the side of the stage, recite a few lines about the history of hula dancing and manage to not throw up!

On the night of the talent show I was sure I would faint. The gym's bleachers at the hosting junior high school were packed with family, friends, and a sizable number of hecklers! Troop #17 was listed midway through the program. With every passing act, I became more panicky. I looked ridiculous in the crepe paper and yanked on my long hair hoping it would conceal my expansive middle, but it barely covered my plump breasts.

And then their dance began! Troop #17 began to gyrate and sway; I advanced to stage right and actually began to recite my lines. The stage lights blinded me; that was good. I only had a couple of lines to go when suddenly both of my bra straps simultaneously broke. There I stood with boobs exposed. Perhaps that was the first-ever "Wardrobe Malfunction!"

The audience broke into hysterics; Troop #17 slowly stopped dancing and anxiously stared at our leader Lucy. Several of the hula girls started to cry; they thought the audience was laughing at them. I slinked behind the stage curtain and promptly began to vomit!

In the end, the talent show judges felt sorry for Troop #17 and still awarded us our badges, but I had temporarily lost the respect of my fellow troop members. They were angry with me; it really wasn't so much that I'd wrecked the talent show, but because I was fat and had puked! Pre-pubescent girls really can be cruel and catty! It took several months to re-earn some credibility with the troop. Known as "the funny girl," I relied on self-deprecating humor to get back into Troop #17's good graces...just in time for summer camp!

Girl Scout Camp turned out to be my last, best effort to bond with my peers. The Girl Scouts owned a camp in a wilderness area of Michigan; it was located about 70 miles from home. Nestled in the pines on a small lake, the camp included a large log cabin dormitory, a kitchen with running water, a mess hall, and even bathrooms and showers. It was actually quite plush for a camp. I was very excited but also terrified. I had never spent the night away from home, and this would be a three-day adventure.

The promise of campfire-storytelling, star gazing, and making s'mores helped quell my apprehension. With my sleeping bag and a backpack that held my brand new Girl Scout Mess Kit, I bravely boarded the bus that fateful Wednesday morning. I didn't even make it to dinner!

I had just claimed a bunk and unloaded my gear when a bee stung me. I am allergic to bees and quickly began to swell. One of the volunteer moms dialed my parents; apparently in the 50s dialing 911 was not yet an option. I sat with my left arm immersed in ice; the rest of the troop ate dinner.

My parents careened around the back roads and arrived before dusk- I was loaded into the back seat of the family car with my sleeping bag, backpack and brand new Girl Scout Mess Kit. The family flew down the back roads to civilization and the closest ER.

I was not a quitter. In the fall of 6th grade I made a second attempt at camp. It turned out to be a similar scenario. This time, during the afternoon whittling session (the scouts were whittling sticks for the promised marshmallows), my knife slipped and I whittled off a small chunk of my knee, and it bled a lot. Once again, my parents were summoned. The ER recognized the family!

My third and final Girl Scout camp-out took place that following spring. Things started out well enough. I made it through dinner and got to finally use my official Girl Scout Mess Kit. I made it through the after-dinner campfire storytelling, and I even got to eat some s'mores; they were delicious!

Obviously the victims of too much sugar, all the girls were running wild in the dormitory, throwing pillows, making scary animal sounds, and giggling. With some considerable effort, I hoisted myself to the top bunk. I had never before had the opportunity to see the world from above. I sprawled out to see if the mattress would be comfy; this was going to be fun!

Unfortunately, a giggling girl in the lower bunk decided to kick the bottom of the top bunk. Unprepared for the unexpected jolt, I flew off of the top bunk and landed squarely on my back. It knocked the wind out of me.

Lucy Jones lost it! She called my mom and dad and tearfully proclaimed, "We fear she may have broken her back!" Well, that got them to the camp in record time; by now my father was familiar with those back roads! I was now able to talk, but the adults would not allow me to sit upright. My back didn't hurt much, but my right thumb throbbed! With some effort, my father and mother half-carried and half-dragged me to the car.

Dad had already notified the ER and off we sped. After many X-rays at the ER, it was determined that my back was fine, but I had broken my right thumb. This almost pleased me, because it excused me from an upcoming piano recital. Still, I never made it through a complete night at Girl Scout camp!

The following week we received a painful call; Lucy Jones resigned as Troop #17's leader. Her husband had supposedly received a promotion and her family would soon re-locate to the East Coast. I just didn't have the energy to get accustomed to yet another leader. Why bother; I had had marginal success in the Girl Scouts.

To date my finest accomplishment was that I had won first prize in the annual Girl Scout cookie sale. It really didn't count though. My mother had bought all of my boxed cookies... my favorites were *Thin Mints* and *Savannahs.*

During the 50s, children did not fare well with rudeness, refusal, obstinacy, or stubbornness; most parents simply would not tolerate it! I couldn't just say, "Forget it! I quit!" It was not my decision to make. I carefully mulled over the possibilities and devised a strategy to soften my parents.

At dinner I broke into fake tears and, with crossed fingers, told mom and dad that I really wanted to focus all of my attention on refining my piano skills. I blubbered that Girls Scouts simply took too much of my time away from piano practice. And then added that I was always afraid I might break another appendage at one of the Girl Scout outings and it might permanently damage my piano playing abilities.

Mother viewed me with a skeptical eye, but my rantings struck a harmonious chord with my father. As an accomplished violinist by avocation, he envisioned us intertwined in a violin/piano concerto on stage! How grand that would be! He quickly aligned with me, and mother lost the battle. By another family vote of 2 to 1, I was allowed to retire from the Girl Scouts. Little did I know that I was now headed for another series of unfortunate events. But that's another story!

As a Fat Girl,
Am I Worthy of Love?
Chapter 5

Nestled within my corpulent frame, beat a seething heart beat for my next-door neighbor. Tom and I had been friends since I was a small child. He was an only child and lived just a few doors away. Daily, he would appear at our back door, greet my mom and sister and then we'd head downstairs to our finished basement den and listen to the latest show tunes and comedians. He often draped his arm around my shoulder as we tuned into our favorites. We never tired of listening to Rita Moreno in *"West Side Story"* and we felt that we belonged to the Jets, because, as you know, "When you're a Jet you're a Jet all the way!" We also loved to listen to the latest comedy albums: The Smothers Brothers and Shelly Berman were among our favorites.

Tom usually stayed for lunch, and Rusty, his loyal Irish setter, would faithfully nap on our back stoop. Tom's mother was a bit of a socialite, and was either golfing, shopping, or sipping! My mom, however, was a Caucasian Aunt Jemima. She loved to cook, clean and stay home. Tom enjoyed being with my family and we all enjoyed Tom; we were inseparable.

During summers, Tom always spent at least two weeks with me at my family's lake home. It was a comfy, old lakefront house located on a beautiful, large, crystal clear lake about 30 miles from our home in town.

There, Tom and I really enjoyed life! We swam, hung out on our float, water skied, sailed, boated, walked, played cards, hunted snapping turtles, and walked to the local marina for calorie-laden treats! It was an idyllic time!

However, as we grew older, I found myself eyeing Tom's maturing physique, and each day I breathed in his delicious cologne! Plus Tom never made fun of my tautly stretched swimsuit or teased me about my weight. He liked me just the way I was. It was a chubby, young teen's fantasy dream!

As we approached puberty, life began to slowly change. I noticed things about Tom that I'd never really paid serious attention to when we were younger. For example, the smell of his cologne, *English Leather,* was a potent aphrodisiac, of the time. Tom was a year younger than I, but he was well built, muscular, and he smelled great! At school he became a major heartthrob of all the girls!

Still, we continued on with our friendship, though I began to feel something in the pit of my obese frame. Love? Lust? Jealousy? Meanwhile, we acquired a new neighbor with a daughter who was in Tom's class at school. Alice was cute, chic, slim, and aloof; I instantly loathed her! Alas, my crush was quickly crushed. Alice won! Still, Tom and I maintained a strong friendship. We did homework together, played Chess, and continued to listen to musicals and comedians. However, at school I remained non-existent!

Worse than that, Tom and Alice had now become boyfriend and girlfriend. I was devastated, but couldn't muster up the necessary pluck to confront him. After all, as an overweight teen, I didn't feel I had the right to confront Tom.

Obviously, Alice was more worthy of his love than I was; and so I remained his "forbidden love!" We continued to study together, laugh together, and enjoy each other's company.

One day during my sophomore year in high school, Tom took it to the next awkward level. He held my hand, walked me over to the sofa and told me to lie down; I did. Then he lowered his fully clothed body on top of me; he didn't move a muscle; he just buried his face in my neck. Unmoving, we stayed in that clumsy position for about fifteen, sweaty minutes. When he stood up I detected a tear running down his face. An Innocent, I feared I might be pregnant. What did I know? Was that why Tom was tearful?

To be sure, I knew absolutely nothing about sex and truly feared I might be pregnant, but the spirit world's Ouija Board guided me directly to "NO!" In retrospect, here are some possibilities about what that day might have actually meant:

- Tom was attempting to practice on his next maneuver with Alice.
- Tom truly liked me but wasn't able to overcome the fear of liking a pudgy girl.
- Tom was overly tired and I was a convenient pillow!

In spite of that outrageous day, our friendship continued to thrive. When my family moved to California during my senior year, Tom often called me and even flew to California for my graduation. By then, I'd lost 60 pounds and Tom now saw me through rose-colored glasses. However my self-confidence had grown too, so Tom and I remained just friends!

The next time I saw Tom was 35 years later. My aging father and I, along with my older sister, made a reunion trip to Michigan. Once we got to Kalamazoo, we set up a time to meet with Tom. He had taken over his father's typewriter business from the '60s and had reconfigured it into the city's only major computer store. He had recently been named "Business Man of the Year" and he was financially secure. Tom had not been lucky in love. He had married and divorced twice. His aging mother was still alive, living in her original home, and Tom provided for her.

And, yes, my heart did skip a beat. He still wore "English Leather!" And, I had been luckier in love than he. My husband and I had been married over thirty year, at that point. However, I still don't know if Tom thought I was worthy! We did enjoy a cup of coffee together and reminisced about our teenage friendship. We parted with a tender kiss and a lingering hug. Maybe I was worthy!

Tell Someone Who Cares!
Chapter 6

I enjoyed a gleeful childhood. The youngest of three children, I learned early in life how to be the perfect child; I was adored by my parents and siblings. Relatives fussed and cooed over me, but I took my good fortune in stride. I naively assumed that the world rightly revolved around me, and I thought life was like that for everyone. I was plump and pretty, with rosy-colored cheeks; I always had a twinkle in my wide, blue eyes and a giggle on my lips!

My older brother adored me; he was 17 years my senior and watched me grow with almost fatherly pride. Often, he would take me along with him to the MIT college library to study. Some skeptics felt he did this to lure coeds to his study nook.

My sister was 11 years older, but she welcomed her little sister into her life; in fact, by choice, we even roomed together! My parents fawned over me and relaxed their former stern parenting notions. It was believed that I was miraculously brought to them to reunite the family! And, it's true; I spent a great deal of time cheering others and making them laugh. I was witty, precocious, and just plain lovable.

As I approached puberty, my role as family clown evolved to family mediator. My new role was more troublesome because family members were always at odds. Still, I had a way about me that could transform a nasty fight into a hilarious exchange of opinions. I was a master of mimicry and could understand the nuances of the personalities that had led to the screaming matches.

All it took was a few well-thought out sentences and my ready smile and impish giggle to make my family take pause and see the humor in the situation. Sometimes though, at night, I was awakened by my parents' nasty, shrill verbal battles. It saddened me because I couldn't always make it right!

My teen years brought some ups and downs. What can I say? I was a typical teenager. I struggled with my blossoming weight, studied hard at school, played the piano, began to admire the opposite sex, had many friends, and sometimes thought my entire family was just plain stupid! However, my role as family mediator was deeply entrenched within me and I continued to be the peacemaker.

In fact, the role expanded to my outside world, as well. My reputation as a funny, witty young lady continued to grow as I aged. I had no enemies, which is unusual for a teenage girl! But sometimes, during the night, I wished I didn't always have to wear my happy face and I would cry and fret about others' nasty behaviors and predicaments!

The clown's path is not always an easy road! I would lie awake and try to think about what funny thing I could do or say to make people happy. More often than not, I would succeed and peace would again return to my valley.

The years passed, my clown-like persona matured as I aged, and my weight continued to fluctuate with each passing dilemma. As an adult I continued to be a "people pleaser." I relied on my self-deprecating humor, hid my personal frustrations and doubts, and I always rolled with the punches! At work I was a team player; I had the ability to work with everyone, both at home and at the office. Well liked, even loved by peers and family, I still continued to play the role cast to me early in life.

It's taken me more than 50 years and several remarkable personal challenges to realize that I am not responsible for everyone else's happiness.

I might be better served to focus on my own needs. What a revelation! How it freed me!

And so it is now, though still with some effort, I actually have the courage to tell a friend or family member that they will simply need to, "Deal with it!" My new mantra, a personal favorite is, "Tell someone who cares!" But as we know, perceptions are often viewed as reality; I will eternally be perceived as a cheerful, plump, caring and always funny lady.

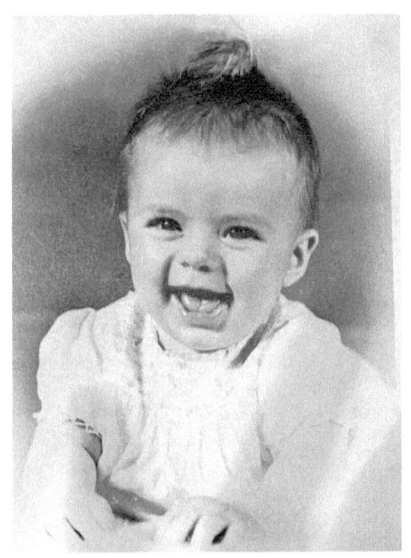

They say I'm adorable enough
to be a Gerber's baby!

My grandma and me.

Every one thinks I'm pretty cute!

Would you like a snack, too?

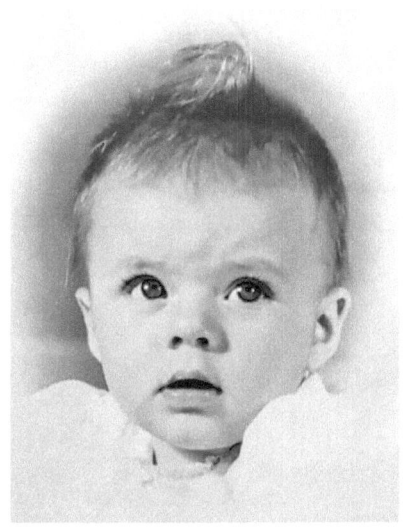

Formula again?

How do I get to the beach?

Read me another story, please!

Work, work, work! I will help dad rake.

What do you think?

I am very pretty in my Sunday best!

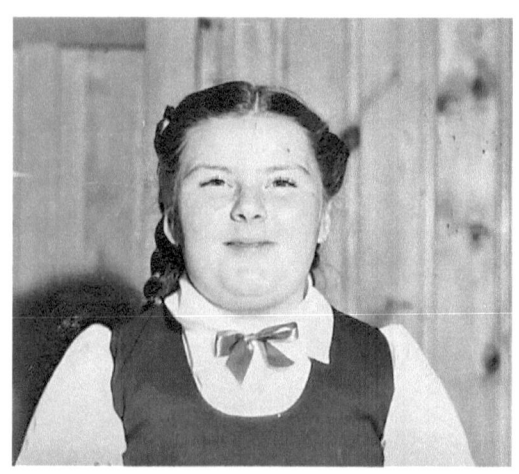

I know a secret!

I've lost so much weight!

College, here I come!

The University of Redlands is my
new home and I love it!

Me posing with my best buds!

The honeymoon is about to begin!

The honeymoon is over already?

Wedding garb in the 70s. Were we hippies?

This cake looks yummy!

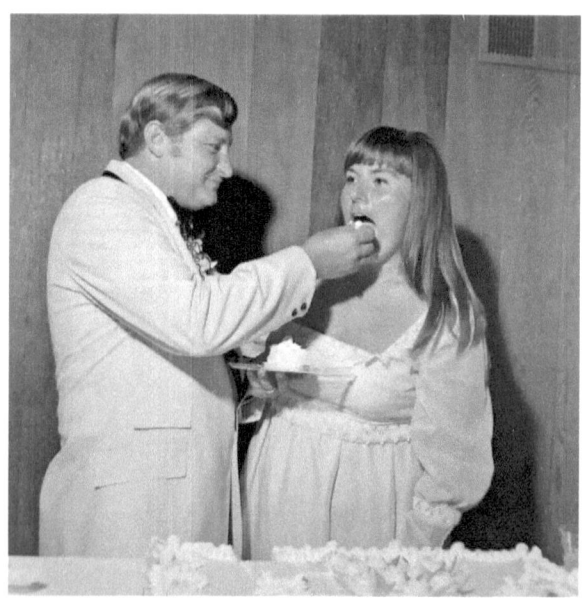

Later, he shoved a piece into my face!

Here we are as young newlyweds.

We are certainly both heavier, but we always have fun!

Who's behind those Foster Grants?

We're adding a Jacuzzi to our home!

Plump again, but I love teaching!

Somebody needs to go on a diet!

Let's sing Christmas carols, in German!

I read the class a scary story by Poe.

Is it Friday, yet?

I'm the V.I.P. at my 73rd birthday!

Bill celebrates another birthday
as he recovers from a broken hip.

Married for 49 years and still smooching!

My Year in Purgatory
Chapter 7

I decided not to call this story **THE YEAR FROM HELL.** Some good things actually did happen, too. Once I had actually survived the fall semester of 1964, my life steadily improved. It was my senior year, and I was attending high school in Portage, Michigan. My father had been offered a wonderful new job in California, and he'd accepted. My life changed!

We would be moving to California, but certainly my parents wouldn't want me to transfer for my senior year in high school! **WRONG!** I pleaded with my folks to let me stay in Michigan for my senior year and suggested that I'd move in with my big sister.

To me it seemed a perfect solution. Joan was eleven years older than I and she taught in a neighboring school district. However, my rigid, German parents refused to even think about it. Years later I learned that my folks had thought Joan had several questionable failings that might corrupt me. Their observations were correct!

The **ONLY** positive was that I assumed the entire state of California was on the ocean. Geography had never been my strong suit! I imagined I might morph into a Sandra Dee-like, bikini-clad beach bunny! **WRONG AGAIN!**

My parents and I left Michigan in late June of 1964. It was a tear-filled departure; I pretty much sobbed until we hit the Missouri state line. My father wouldn't allow me to listen to the "crap" on the radio, so I silently hummed Chuck Berry's hit, "Get Your Kicks on Route 66." I felt it was more like "Get Kicked in the Gut on Route 66."

It was a long trek for a teenager and I was miserable! My family did not travel well. My mom always had trouble getting started in the morning. My father would clearly tell us that we would promptly leave from the motel by 7:00 a.m. Unfortunately, that meant that if dad were lucky, we might leave by 10:00 a.m. And so, it took forever to traverse this nation.

Occasionally, my mom would break out into song; usually she would sing "America The Beautiful." When she was truly moved, she would belt out Kate Smith's rendition of "God Bless America." My mother was a true fan of Kate Smith's radio show. They were approximately the same age. They were both large, corpulent women. They both were viewed, at least in public settings, as content, happy, and wholesome ladies. But I digress... back to our journey.

Each day on the road, my father drove like a crazy man to make up the lost miles from my mother's late starts. Much to my mother's dismay, he would whiz by all historical landmarks, antique shops, souvenir stops, and lookout points. And, daily, we went through a ritual to find a suitable motel with vacancies.

I was assigned to go through the AAA Triptik to find a motel, maybe with a swimming pool. Each night we would get lost and by the time we actually got to our rooms, the motels' swimming pools were already closed for the night. We were on the road for six or seven days and as we raced past any historical or interesting sights, we saw only occasional coffee shops and dreary motel rooms along Route 66.

It didn't dawn on me until we had entered the state of California that I was roasting in the desert heat. We stopped in Barstow to get some gas. I remember opening the car door and all the oxygen was immediately sucked out of my lungs. It was 116 degrees! This can't be; where the hell is the ocean? I had seen a sign saying ENTERING SAN BERNARDINO COUNTY! My father had told me earlier that Redlands, our new home, was located in San Bernardino County. I became weak in the knees; my life was over! I wanted to cry, but I was too dehydrated and no tears fell.

The ride from Barstow to Redlands was brutal. I wanted to be anywhere but where I was. Normally, I would have been frolicking with my friends in the lake at my family's Michigan summer home. Instead, I was imprisoned in the back seat of a dark red, 1964 Oldsmobile.

My dad had already found a temporary home to lease. As we entered Redlands, I was surprised to see a lot of greenery in this small, quaint little town. Apparently Redlands was desert adjacent; still, it was very hot, but humans could actually survive there!

As we drove up the long driveway to our new home, I saw a small orange grove to my right. Ahead of me was a rambling, L- shaped ranch style home with floor-to-ceiling glass windows. There was also a huge bay window that provided panoramic views of the town below and the mountain ranges in the distance.

As I took a tour of our new home with my folks, I realized it was very contemporary and expansive. There was even a huge swimming pool and pool house that was cantilevered over the canyon behind the house. We would be living in style, but who cared?

It turned out that the home's owner was one of the "Angels of Bataan" who had written about her struggles as a nurse and World War II war prisoner in the Pacific. She had built this home with the proceeds from her book. The house's study was wall papered with World War II Pacific maps; even the ceiling was covered in maps. I have no idea why she chose to lease it to us, but now it had become our new, temporary home.

The next day, the moving van arrived with all of our possessions. The reality hit me hard. Not even my prized canopy bed made me smile. I was very nostalgic about leaving behind most everyone who meant anything to me. And, I became nauseous every time I thought about what my new school would be like.

My ONLY friend that summer was my beagle Tippy. He had flown to California and been spared the cross-country trek. Always a faithful dog, he knew just when to nuzzle me and lick my face. He was adjusting to California better than I was!

He loved the new smells and scenery to explore. He even had his own digs! There was a small, walled-in corral at the top of the driveway and adjacent to our carport. Tippy was in doggy heaven;

even when he was assigned to the corral, there was plenty of room to roam and sniff. Plus, he could sit on the top of the corral wall and bay at strange vermin in the canyon behind the house. He was one, happy dog!

I remained sullen and weepy for the rest of that summer. My only solace... **FOOD**. I pretty much munched my way through August. My main diversions were Tippy, the pool, and the refrigerator... at least until we found a full-sized rattlesnake gently skimming through the pool water.

It turned out that there was a large nest of rattlesnakes living beneath the pool. It was shady and cool there and they were quite content. First, my dad used a long hook to capture our guest rattlesnake. Next, he grabbed his shotgun and accidently peppered the entire fiberglass wall of the pool, but the snakes remained entrenched. Finally, he called the Animal Control and asked for **HELP!**

Of course, it took me several days to feel brave enough to venture back to the pool. Animal Control had captured and removed the nest, but I was still quite leery. Only my mom would brazenly walk barefoot out the back door to the pool and defiantly exclaim, "If the Good Lord brought me all the way to California to get snake-bit, then so be it!" There are more snake stories I will tell you about later.

My mom had more moxie than I. I need to take a few minutes to adequately describe my mother. She was a first-born daughter, born two months after my grandparents immigrated to America. My grandmother was German and my grandfather was French. Mom had two younger sisters and my mom and her family lived in what today would be called a Chicago ghetto.

My grandma was a drunk and my granddad died from diphtheria when my mom was only six. Mom had trouble with the nuns at school because she spoke a kind of fractured German/English mix.

After my grandpa died, my grandma took in borders. She was a seamstress, and drank a good deal. My mom and her sisters pretty much spent each afternoon sitting in the Catholic Church waiting for my grandma to take them home.

The nuns often dropped in to see what my grandma was cooking for dinner and occasionally brought the family a scrawny chicken to throw into the pot. They were not very charitable, certainly no angels of mercy!

The tale of how my parents met is worthy of yet another book. My dad, born on a farm in Wisconsin, was the youngest of nine boys. He was the only son born in America. He had hoped to become a violinist, but in 1928, the year my parents wed, there was not a huge demand for violinists. He had no formal schooling but decided to pursue aeronautical engineering. He became one of our nation's top scientists, and he was self-taught. He was definitely a genius; the violin remained his passionate avocation.

My mom dutifully stuck by his side and we moved to wherever my father thrived. She was living an adventuresome life for a shoeless waif from Chicago. Mom cooked and cleaned; she starched and ironed dad's shirts; she patiently listened to my dad's professional rants; and she happily listened to my father play his violin at all hours of the day or night. As the family moved from coast to coast, mom got to see most of our great nation.

I will always remember my mom as a Caucasian Aunt Jemima who spoke English with German word order. She was extremely heavy set and usually wore a simple housedress and apron; she always wore a kerchief on her head as she vacuumed and cleaned.

We lived well, though many of our snooty neighbors thought she was the maid or cook. My mom was very proud of her home and my father. However, she often was intimidated because of her size and lack of formal education. Still, she was extremely well read and remained eager and willing to learn new things. Enough said... now you have a better understanding of my family's dynamics.

Late in August I had my first glimpse of my new high school where I was told to report for registration. I couldn't believe it... RHS was a sprawling, single story campus with covered walkways. In Michigan, because of the inclement weather, schools were self-contained, multi-story buildings. Only the gym and possibly the Performing Arts Theater would be housed in separate buildings. In Michigan I had been enrolled in Advanced Placement (AP) classes. There was no such thing at RHS. Also, they had no advanced German classes, so I ended up with French I.

However, the most astonishing thing that I saw that day was how the female students dressed! In Michigan, all the girls wore dresses or pleated wool skirts (no slacks allowed). *Bass Weejun* penny loafers with knee socks were the hot fashion trend!

Here, the girls were wearing tottering heels or strappy sandals, slinky dresses, skin-tight pencil skirts with taut tank tops and OMG... a garment that was called panty hose! Also, the girls wore heavy makeup, a trend that had been shunned at my former high school.

Also, on registration day I saw my first Mexican girl fight! I was so shocked I couldn't move; I actually sat down on the pavement to watch. The fight spread and soon there were about twenty Mexican American girls ripping out each other's hair and screaming obscenities. A guidance counselor grabbed me and pulled me out of the way to safety.

I soon learned that these spontaneous brawls often broke out on campus, usually at lunch or after school; often the guys would fight, too. Those fights got serious; guys were frequently hurt. However, the Mexican girls were more flamboyant and meaner! They would go after each other for just about anything: dirty looks; cheating boyfriends; shades of fingernail polish; whacky hairstyles; or mean, sideways glances! However, boys and family were the biggest reasons to fight and the girls seemed more vicious!

Anyway... Now I was not only lonely, I also feared for my life! I really didn't want to spend my senior year worrying about walking across campus or going to the bathroom! All I could think to do that quieted my *Angst* was to eat! And, so I ate, and ate, and ate! By the time school even began I was heavier than I had ever been and my bathing suit was stretched to its limits.

On the first day of school, I boarded the mostly vacant school bus, moved to the back and sat down. The bus slowly filled as we drove along the Redland's famed, scenic Sunset Drive. The bus jerked to another stop. Two older, male teens boarded the bus. One pointed towards the back of the bus and blurted, "Check out the fat girl with the big nose!" I swung around to see about whom he was talking. I realized he was pointing directly at me! Total humiliation before I had even gotten off that bus. Welcome to RHS!

I followed my class schedule by the hour. There were no familiar, friendly faces to acknowledge with a smile or a wave. It seemed like it was me against the entire world! By lunchtime I was ravenous! As I moved along the cafeteria line, I grabbed almost every available calorie-laden dish, sat down by myself and inhaled my lunch. The food was not that tasty, but it was plentiful!

Refortified, I stared across the busy cafeteria. I had read about their sacred "R" crest in the center of the room. It was a tradition that NOBODY was ever to step on the revered crest. The Devil took over my body. I jumped up, grabbed my books and purposely stomped and re-stomped across that stupid crest. The cafeteria quieted. I had intentionally committed a dastardly act! I didn't know how to react. Apparently that stupid crest actually did have meaning for these kids. I had crossed the line and the die was cast. I was, officially, a kid to be loathed!

My classes were so easy. I never had to study and aced every test I took. My fellow classmates were pissed! I was screwing up the curve! The teachers thought I was a genius. Truth be told, I had been a struggling student in Michigan. There was stiff academic pressure, and class standards and curricula were tougher to master.

In Redlands, fellow students didn't aspire to improving their grades. Their social lives were their main focus. And, I had repeatedly flunked in any social setting. Plus, now I was way past "borderline obese" and I hated my nose! I asked my mom if I could have a nose job. In her typically German fashion she quickly blurted, "How would you like it if you didn't even have a nose!" That meant, NO!

In order to cheer me up, my father bought me a new, white, 1964 Nash-Rambler convertible.. Naturally, I was not included in the decision-making process. After all, it was 1964. He bought a convertible, but with the top down, it resembled a rolling bathtub. It was absolutely not a "hot" car. I felt like I needed a shower cap on hot days. Really, nobody wanted a friend who drove a Nash-Rambler! My father took it to work one day and had a freeway collision. My father walked away with just a few scrapes; however the car was totaled. I was thrilled it was no longer a part of my personal life!

Some things were good, though. I got to reestablish my loving relationship with my big brother in California. Joe, seventeen years my senior, was an aeronautical engineer. He was going through a divorce and had three darling, young children. We quickly reconnected. I adored my big brother. He was witty, bright, light-hearted, and charismatic!

By Christmas I had ballooned to 260+ pounds. At a family gathering, Joe took me aside for a heart-to-heart conversation. He told me that underneath the fat, I was a very pretty girl and if I lost some weight, things would get better. He said that in college life would vastly improve. He told me that if I lost weight, he would buy me a ski outfit and take me skiing in Mammoth. You need to know that if Joe had told me to stand on my head in a corner for an entire year, I would have done just that!

I officially announced my weight loss goal at the start of Lent. I gave up just about everything. I rejected my mom's daily pleas to just "eat a little something" and the pounds started to peel off. Mom told me that on Sundays during Lent, one could indulge in whatever one had given up. I'm not sure if that was an official church ruling or a "mom" rule, but it worked for me. On Sundays I would indulge in a candy bar, cookies, or ice cream.

And then on Monday I was ready to refrain for the rest of the new week

I faithfully followed that Lent diet until graduation. I had shed over seventy pounds, and by the time I entered college that fall, I was down to 142 pounds. We never made it to Mammoth; instead, Joe bought me a cool swimsuit and took me sailing!

I can't say my life at RHS greatly improved, but people did begin to notice me with a wave or smile. I was feeling much better about myself; my self-esteem had slowly returned. I was even asked to the prom, but I turned it down. Instead, on prom night, and with one of my few pals, I rushed to see the Rolling Stones at the San Bernardino County Fairgrounds! It was my first rock concert!

Of course, my life was still far from perfect. My classmates still didn't appreciate me. Though I had earned a straight 4.0 GPA, apparently they did not consider that a good thing! Also now my folks and I were bickering about colleges. I wanted to go to Michigan State or the U of M. They said it was too far away from home and demanded I stay nearby! I refused to apply in state and just shut down. I remember my dad saying, "Good! I'll just buy you a fruit stand to work... it's much cheaper!"

Graduation Day was more of a relief than a festive occasion. It took place at the Redlands Bowl, an outdoor amphitheater in town. It was early evening, but still very warm. My sister had flown in from Michigan. My mom, dad, Joe, Joan and my eldest niece Karen were there!

The ceremony meant little to me, I just wanted out. A fellow senior had invited me to Grad Night. He was cute enough, but no mental giant! He ate his way through Disneyland, and by the time we got home, I was beyond exhausted!

I forgot to tell you about my near-death experience on graduation day. I had just driven home from rehearsal and I saw dad's car in the driveway. I knew that meant he had just picked up Joan from the airport. In my zeal to greet her, I forgot to put the car into park or shut off the engine as I pulled into the carport. As I leaned across the front seat to roll up the window, I noticed the car was slowly inching forward. Instead of hitting the brakes, I panicked and pumped the accelerator. I drove through the back wall of the carport. The car's back wheels lodged on the short cement retaining wall and the car teetered on the edge of the canyon. I had to crawl out the back seat.

My father ran out of the front door. He thought there had been an explosion in the canyon. He looked at me standing in the driveway and then looked at his prized, new Oldsmobile teetering precariously on the small retaining wall. The hood was covered with the flowery bougainvillea remains from the carport trellis.

My father, normally a heavy swearer, was too stunned to utter even one cuss word! The day before, he had had the car serviced and realigned. We were to drive back to Michigan for the summer, and he had wanted the car to be in prime condition for the journey.

Dad walked into the house and called AAA. When the truck arrived, the repairmen were stunned. Finally, they broke into laughter, but soon realized my dad was not amused! It took some time, but by using a hoist, they were finally able to lift the car off of that wall. The day after graduation, dad was at the dealer by 8:00 a.m. to make some cosmetic touch-ups and re-realign the car. I figured it was a done deal.

Unfortunately, there were repercussions. Mom and dad decided that I was to hand over all of the money that had been gifted to me for graduation. My brother had given me $200 as a gift; sadly the money was earmarked for the repair of the garage. Still, I knew I would soon be heading back to Michigan and my friends, so that soothed my empty wallet!

Two days later at around 10:30 a.m. (mom was winning!), we finally pulled out of the driveway bound for Michigan. I was so excited that time seemed to fly. In the back seat, Joan and I gossiped and giggled our way across the country. As we neared Michigan, my excitement grew.

Finally we pulled into the side yard of my family's summer cottage. It looked a little over-run by weeds and fallen branches, but to me, I had just re-entered my former life and it was beautiful! It was exhilarating! I couldn't wait to contact my friends but, of course, we're talking about the pre-cell phone era! I needed to wait until my parents ordered our landline to be reactivated. To them, it was not a big deal, but I thought I would lose my mind!

We crashed that first night in our old, familiar cottage beds. It was absolute heaven and I fell asleep to the gentle lapping of the waves hitting against the rock break wall. The next morning every family member was assigned a cleanup duty. Joan worked with my father on the outdoors clean up and my mother and I worked cleaning up the inside of the cottage. The outside took longer to restore, but by day's end, the only three remaining chores were to clean out all the cottage gutters, to get our boat out of storage and re-launched, and to drag our massive float back into the water.

Michigan winters are historically brutal. Gull Lake is a beautiful, large inland lake and it's over six miles long and up to 90 feet deep. The winter ice can reach up to six feet thick, so everything needs to be removed from the lake early each fall. The only heat we had at our cottage was the fireplace. We rarely went there during winters! And, it was an absolute necessity to remove the float from the lake each autumn.

By our third day, everything was refreshed and restored; I was ready to take control of my summer! The landline had been reactivated; I was able to catch up with all my former friends. It was a magical summer, and each passing day was spent frolicking with friends, sunbathing and boating. They were all impressed with my weight loss! The horrors of my senior year began to wash away in the lake water. I swam, I water skied, I sailed. It was idyllic!

For a brief period of time, I was able to push away my nagging fears about college. But as the summer progressed, I realized that all of my close friends would soon be leaving for college, while I had no idea about what would be my fate! My folks allowed me to stay in Michigan for the entire summer. Dad's vacation was almost over, but they did agree to let me spend the remaining few summer weeks at the lake with Joan.

Of course, all of my Michigan friends were heading to either Michigan State in Lansing or the U of Michigan in Ann Arbor. And I hadn't even applied to one school. In a last ditch effort to remain in Michigan, I called my parents in California to see if they might allow me to stay in Michigan if I chose a Catholic girls' college to attend.

For years I had studied piano at Nazareth, a Catholic girls' college on the outskirts of Kalamazoo. My parents were actually receptive. They figured the campus had ten feet tall walls to keep me safe and pure! Little did they know that many girls in private schools were notoriously wild and wanton!

Two days later I received an alarming, long distance phone call from my brother. In summary, he told me to forget about going to a Catholic girls' college. He said he had watched our sister's demise as a result of a private girls' college. He was not about to lose his little sister, too. He told me to get my butt onto a plane and return to California and that he'd help me find a school that would take me at such a late date. As I've told you before, Joe was my hero, and so I packed and was soon headed back to California!

Once home, Joe and I put our heads together and applied to the University of Redlands, a small, private, liberal arts college; it was affiliated with the Baptist Church. My Catholic parents didn't even care that it was a Baptist college; at least it was local. Joe figured since my parents were Redlands residents, the school might take a second look at me. Meanwhile, time was running out; it was the third week of August!

As a Plan B Option, Joe made me enroll at the local junior college in San Bernardino. I actually attended classes there for two very long days. I was absolutely miserable. It was nothing more than a high school with ashtrays. That second afternoon, I received a late afternoon call from the U of R Admissions Office; they had found an opening for me. I was to report for school the next day.

I was ecstatic! Even though I had missed most of Frosh Orientation, there were still a couple of days to get acclimated to my new life at college before classes began!

True, there were a few negatives:
- I wasn't in Michigan.
- The university was in the same town that my parents lived.

- They didn't have a dorm room available, so I would need to live at home for at least one semester.

However, there were some, positives, too:
- It wasn't a junior college.
- All the freshmen students seemed bright and friendly.
- And, most importantly, there were lots of very cute boys!

Once I had a class schedule and classes had begun, I realized the U of R was a perfect fit for me! I finally understood that my parents had been correct; a large university would have swallowed me. **My year in Purgatory was finally over!** I felt truly happy; I had lost weight; I loved my courses; I started dating; and life was so much better!

Where Would You Like It, Sir?
Chapter 8

I really didn't need to work during the summers. In fact, my parents discouraged me. They hoped I would stay home, practice piano, spend time reading the classics and, of course, continue my studies in German. They could well afford to subsidize me and hated the thought of me doing menial labor.

As I am sure you can imagine, I would have preferred any job to staying home! The problem was that I really had no marketable skills. In high school I was too busy taking honors and Advanced Placement courses to have room in my schedule for anything as mundane as typing. (These days, of course, the computer has replaced typing!)

However, the summer following my freshman year in college, I did discover one possibility; I could become a waitress. My parents were appalled, but undaunted I hit the pavement and on the very first day, I landed a job as a waitress in a pizza parlor!

That summer was my first encounter with the real world. I spent the summer in Michigan and lived with my older sister in a small, second story, studio apartment. In addition to working, I was also enrolled in a French class at the local university. That summer I learned a lot about the harsh realities of life and also how to conjugate French verbs.

To begin with, I was the only coed at the restaurant. The other waitresses were divorced mothers trying to put food on the table for their children. None of these ladies appreciated a sweet, plump, young coed competing for tips! Early on, I had made the fatal mistake of telling the staff that I was working to save money for a semester of study in Europe.

These hardened divorcees made life very difficult for me: they would take my entrees to one of their tables and then blame me for the order screw up; they would pay the busboy extra tips if he didn't clean my tables; they frequently told our boss that I was a hopeless case.

Once, they even locked me into the walk-in-freezer. Fortunately Pancho, the night cook, heard a muffled scream and set me free. Of course, he hoped to be rewarded for his daring rescue, and that became yet another obstacle; I had to out-maneuver his roving hands.

The customers were not much nicer. The pizza house, unimaginatively called the **House of Pizza,** happened to be located adjacent to the Greyhounds

Bus Depot in Kalamazoo, Michigan. What can I say? It definitely lacked a certain *je ne sais pas qui*. Our clientele consisted mainly of weary, down-and-out travelers; tired, grumpy, overweight bus drivers; an occasional vagrant and an assortment of army GIs heading home on leave. Mostly, they all hated me. I was entirely too perky and college-like for this seedy crowd. The tips were horrid except for a few horny soldiers who hoped I served more than pizza and left larger tips to attest their interest.

The food, if not gourmet, was presented in generous portions! We served pizza, assorted Italian pasta dishes and even offered a tasty, but greasy roasted chicken with French fries. Of course, spumoni ice cream, tapioca or bread pudding were also available for an extra 75 cents.

My primary goal was to keep my parents out of the restaurant if they did return to Michigan that summer! My secondary goal was to survive each night and not overeat. I worked six nights per week. My hours were from 5:00 p.m. to 11:00 p.m.

In those days, I made $1.00 per hour, plus tips. Though my parents had never denied me anything, I soon became addicted to earning my own money. Each night when I returned home, my feet aching, my hair full of grease, and my hands reeking of the vinegar we used to clean down the tables, I would plunk down onto the floor and count the bills and roll the change. On my best night, I earned $38.75 plus my hourly wages; the grand total was $44.75. I was rich!

That summer I learned several valuable lessons that served me well as my waitress career evolved:

1. Keep a low profile about college studies.

2. Beware of career waitresses; they are mean!

3. The busboy can be your best friend; tip him well!

4. Each day tell your customers that it is your very first day. They will feel sorry for you and leave a bigger tip! (This tactic does not work well with repeat customers.)

5. Pretend that you have a very large, muscle-bound, jealous boyfriend. (This strategy works particularly well on cooks, managers and sex-starved customers.)

And, there was one more valuable lesson learned. Following a late night shift at the pizza parlor, I slept through my final exam in French and, as a result, I only received a C- from the French prof. …. too low a grade to transfer to my university in California. I vowed that summer that I would never again take a 7:30 a.m. class!

The following summer I was hired as a waitress at a privately owned coffee shop on Coast Highway in Corona del Mar, a beautiful resort town on the ocean in Orange County, California. I felt very grateful; with my parents' hesitant blessings, I was allowed to live with my older brother and his new bride in their Newport Beach home.

I worked the early shift. The restaurant opened at 6:00 a.m.; that meant that I needed to be there no later than 5:15 a.m. Those who knew me well realized that this would be a shock to my system. I had never been a morning person; I loved to stay up late!

Fortunately, the owner was also not a morning person; in fact, she rarely showed up before 11:00 a.m. As a result, she missed many of my early morning mishaps. I would forget to put the cups in the saucers before I started to pour the coffee. If the Mexican cook put on a pot of *menudo* for himself, I would become nauseated by the smell and frequently gag. I had difficulty carrying more than two plates or two glasses of juice at the same time. It was also difficult for me to remember the menu at that ungodly hour. I tried to apply Lesson # 4 (see above), but it really didn't work. Most of the clients were local yokels and remembered me!

On my second day of work, I survived a horrendous event. The lunch hour was fast approaching. The two chefs cooked behind the counter, exhibition style.

They both wore tall, white, starched chefs' hats and black aprons. In the kitchen, they would starch their hats by putting them over large cans of beans, spraying the hats with spray starch, and setting the hats and cans on the stove shelf above a pot of simmering *soup du jour*. Well, the head chef made the fatal mistake of putting the can of spray starch onto that same shelf. Unfortunately, he set it too close to the edge and the can of spray starch fell into the boiling bean soup.

I was just about to go through the swinging doors into the kitchen when an explosion rocked the restaurant. I was thrown back; customers screamed and ran out of the restaurant. There were beans everywhere; they had blown under the kitchen door and splattered the dining room walls.

I ran into the kitchen and witnessed a terrifying scene. The soup pot had cracked the gas burner and started a fire. I screamed at the busboy to get the fire extinguisher. Much to my dismay, the busboys had been "playing" with the extinguisher the previous day and it was empty.

The cook called the fire department and soon we heard sirens. Meanwhile, the other waitress slipped in the beans, fell and broke her right arm. Shortly after the fire was extinguished, the owner arrived. Her biggest concern was that the customers failed to pay their bills before fleeing for their lives. According to her, the lunch hour receipts were down and it was obviously the waitresses' faults. We were supposed to collect the money as they fled! Did I mention that this coffee shop was not well managed?

Mid-summer I was moved to the dinner shift. Things improved, but the p.m. cook was a frustrated Don Juan. He devoted many hours to try to seduce me with his lurid looks and off-color innuendos. He was particularly fond of grabbing a banana from the fruit bowl and suggestively waving it at me as he slowly stroked it and gave me a knowing look. When we ran out of bananas, a cucumber would do. I became adept at dodging and weaving when Manuel was near.

I became a better waitress that summer. By summer's end, I had mastered the menu and the cash register. I could carry four dinner plates on my arm and avoid any nasty spills. I made a wicked chocolate malt, and I was also well skilled at making banana splits; often though, our bananas were bruised! I endeared myself to the locals and made a lot of money in tips. I was well on my way to my semester abroad!

I reached the pinnacle of my career as a waitress the summer following college graduation. My two roommates and I were back at the beach. We would be attending graduate school at U.C.I. in the fall. I was hired as a cocktail/dinner waitress at a well-known Mexican restaurant in Newport Beach. This was particularly amazing since I knew absolutely nothing about the world of mixed drinks or Mexican food.

I mean, I knew what I liked, but I never knew what was in it! I had no idea whether a drink was to be served with an onion, an olive, a lime, a lemon twist, or a cherry. Waitresses were supposed to call in the drinks by their abbreviated names. For example a "Bloody Mary" would be ordered as a "Mary;" a "Vodka Martini with ice" was to be announced as a "Vodka Marty rocks." I didn't even know the difference between a "Gimlet" and a "Gibson."

I was on a definite learning curve that summer. Plus, as a mid-westerner, I had little knowledge of Mexican cuisine. I couldn't tell an enchilada from a burrito or a taco from a Chile relleno. I couldn't easily recognize the difference between an enchilada or a burrito; they were both smothered in cheese and red or green sauce. I also was slow to see the differences between a taco and a taquito. What did I know about Mexican food? I was from Michigan!

Let's just say I had a great deal to master. Of course, I learned by sampling the menu. Meals were free and I was broke. I gained over thirty pounds that summer and I was, once again, becoming really chubby!

Once again, I was the youngest waitress. In fact two of the older waitresses were both having affairs with the owner. It was really remarkable; these two waitresses would actually fight over who got to wait on the owner and his lovely, French wife when the loving couple arrived for dinner. The owner had three sons; two of them were bartenders, and like their dad, they also had roving eyes and hands.

One of my favorite stories from that summer illustrates my woeful lack of sophistication in my understanding of alcoholic beverages. I served wine and dinner to a middle-aged couple nestled in a dimly-lighted, side booth. As I retrieved their empty plates the gentleman said, "We would like two cups of coffee and some *Anisette*."

Well, I thought he had a headache. I went to the bartender and asked him if we had any *Anacin*. Unfortunately, we only had *Bufferin*. I put the coffee and the *Bufferin* on the tray and walked back to the booth where I apologized profusely for our lack of *Anacin*. I assured him, however, that the *Bufferin* would do the trick. He gave me a cold, icy stare and blurted, "Dear Lady, I said *Anisette*; it's a drink"

I headed back to the bar, but the bartender, a recent graduate from bartending school, was also clueless! He methodically read the Bartender's Guide and then he got out a flashlight. We read through the labels on the bottles behind the bar and eventually discovered that *Ainisette* is a licorice-flavored, after-dinner liqueur. I am not sure who was more relieved: the couple, the bartender, or me!

It was the kind of restaurant where secret lovers would meet in the late afternoon to have drinks and paw their paramours before heading home to their spouses. The lighting was dim and the drinks were generous. The bar was always filled with well-oiled workers and salesmen from the neighboring yacht brokers and boat yards. These guys could drink!

The restaurant included a piano bar that featured Ricardo, the *Mexican Keyboard King*. He could also sing, though he never sang until he had consumed at least three glasses of vodka on the rocks with a lime. With a thick Spanish accent he would lisp through several sultry numbers as his lusty gaze focused on any single woman at the bar. If there were no available, lonely women drinking at the bar, he would pick out one of the waitresses to croon. It was always very embarrassing to be the object of Ricardo's unrequited passion.

The beach crowd was much more sophisticated than the folks I had served at my previous establishments. I learned a new valuable lesson; in general, yuppies and suits tend to believe that all waitresses are stupid and should be treated as such.

As a recent college graduate, I wanted to wear a large billboard sign that confirmed my graduate status. I waited on many customers where I fought the urge to drop their entrees into their laps. With pursed lips I would have first whispered under my breath, "Just where would you like it, Sir!"

Women were the biggest offenders! Most of them were rude, arrogant, demanding, and demeaning. If there was a mistake with their order, they would instantly blame the waitress, and with a wave of the hand, they would demand that the order be immediately returned to the kitchen. In reality, the mistakes were most often committed by the chef who was hooked on tequila shooters. Women also demanded separate checks. Apparently, even though they were all "college graduates" they had never learned how to add or divide.

In spite of the negatives, it was still a good place to work. In those days, it was one of the busiest restaurants at the beach. The owner was very kind to me and treated me like a daughter. He would send me home before the rowdy, late-night crowd arrived, and he favored me with customers whom he recognized as big tippers.

I worked at the restaurant through that winter while I was attending graduate school. I worked as the hostess and was allowed to study when the evening rush had slowed, and he paid me an unheard of $7.00/hour to offset the lost tips! After I had completed my student teaching, I returned to my former position as waitress.

I remained at the restaurant until the following fall when I retired and began my "real" career as a chubby, first year teacher. It was a sad discovery to learn that I made more money as a part-waitress than I did as a beginning teacher!

Family Foibles
Chapter 9

Where to start? Every family has their own brand of hereditary idiosyncrasies. My family offered a plethora of common quirks. The top three shared genetic traits among our family members were obesity, punctuality, and prevication. We all loved to skirt around the truth.

Many in my family struggled with life–long weight battles. Most of my immediate family members were decidedly plump. And, while a few of my closest kin fought the battle daily, none of us ever really maintained what was considered a normal weight.

The story I am about to tell you will provide an example of how my family spent one lovely, summer day. My very obese sister Joan was visiting from Michigan. My chubby father was still dealing with my mom's sudden passing. My plump brother, in an attempt to prevent a drawn-out visit with my grieving father and sister, suggested a ride on a pontoon boat at Big Bear Lake. We all agreed it might be fun.

My brother, a Newport Beach resident, borrowed a van from his employer and he and his wife Carolyn would drive us all up the mountain. We agreed to meet at my father's home in Redlands. Now you need to know that my brother was never punctual. Both he and Carolyn were no slaves to the clock. Carolyn was not overweight, but she could easily become annoyed and we would all hear her grievances of the day... multiple times.

As I said, she was NEVER on time and if we wanted her to be anywhere near being on time, we would give her an hour cushion. If we wanted her to be somewhere by noon, we would tell her the starting time was 11:00. Carolyn, a great cook, had prepared sandwiches, chips, salads, cookies, and beverages. She filled a giant cooler with these treats. Of course that made her run out of time and when they did arrive at my father's, they were forty minutes late.

My father was fuming because he supposedly had made the boat reservation for noon and complained bitterly that we would never make it on time. My sister was already hungry and her blood sugar was plummeting. With some effort we finally got situated in the van and we began our trek to Big Bear. My sister-in-law had already claimed the front passenger seat, supposedly to offset her habitual carsickness tendency. My sister ruffled through bags in search of some calorie-filled treats to offset her growing hunger pangs.

My brother raced up the mountain hoping to make it to the pontoon boat on time. My dad continued to grumble and blame my brother for wrecking the day. My husband Bill and I remained very quiet, hoping to dodge any potential family spats.

As we wound up the mountain, my dad began to giggle; he had a secret that he soon blabbed. He had changed the boat reservation to 1:00 pm; we had plenty of extra time to make it to the marina on time. Obviously, this fact really angered Joe. I do not believe that his blood pressure actually fell!

My sister said that now there was enough time to stop at *Colonel Sanders* to buy some fried chicken for the cruise. Despite the fact that we had a van laden with food, she was insistent that fried chicken was needed. Even though she had only been to Big Bear once before and years ago, she knew exactly where the store was located. After considerable bickering, my father argued that he wanted chicken, too!

Now, getting Joan out of the van took a major effort, but she was a woman on a mission and she soon waddled across the parking lot and into the store. That was a big mistake... she decided that TWO buckets of chicken were what we needed, crispy and extra crispy!

My brother was so enraged; I feared a shootout in the parking lot. There was really not enough room in the van to add two huge buckets of chicken. And the next hurdle was getting my sister back into the van. First, she needed to be able to step up onto the van's running board. Bill and Joe hovered behind her to help her hoist her ample bottom into the van. By the twinkle in Joe's eye, I could tell he was preparing to utter an unkind comment about her, excuse my foul language, "big, fat ass." I nudged them both and whispered, **"DON'T YOU DARE!"**

Finally we arrived at the marina and unloaded the bags of food and the cooler brimming with more food. Next, Joe and my father scrutinized the pontoon boat. Both were aeronautical engineers, and they poked and prodded their way through the boat. Joe determined that the first boat had a bent propeller, so we had to wait while workers finally located a second pontoon boat; it passed my brother's white-glove inspection. Finally we were allowed to board. Getting situated took more time. My sister ripped into the buckets of chicken before we had even left the dock.

What can I say... we ate and ate and ate some more! Carolyn wanted to make sure her sandwiches, salads, chips and drinks were not passed over by Joan's chicken. It was a gorgeous afternoon, but the day revolved solely around food, not the scenery, nor the delightful weather!

We re-docked around 5:00 and slowly shuffled off the boat. Once the van was reloaded, we began our descent down the mountain. We were all in a hyperglycemic stupor.

Carolyn, fighting carsickness, asked to lie down on the floor of the van. My father graduated to the front seat. As we wound down the mountain, only Joan remained animated. I will never forget the question she blurted out. She asked, "Where will we stop for dinner?" She was hit with a resounding, **"NOWHERE... WE'RE GOING HOME!"**

The .05% Factor
Chapter 10

Based on my current age, I was only slim for a relatively short period of time. I was at my most trim during my college days! And, I considered myself to be sizzlin' hot! Who knew that being a normal size was so intoxicating!

I certainly never lacked for dates, and I feasted on the possibilities and smorgasbord of options that called to me! I was so taken with myself, that depending on my mood, I might actually accept two dates for a single day. I was never risqué; I just wanted to be admired. As a college freshman, I still lived at home. I was considered a "local" girl and I believe the college boys who asked me out thought I must be "easy," but I was not!

One Friday night I had a date with Ed, a college junior, and felt truly admired! We had enjoyed a pizza together at the local college haunt; next we headed to the local bowling alley, followed by sipping booze in the bowling alley parking lot.

My family lived high above the town in the prestigious hills of Redlands, CA. Our home had a very long driveway, with a grove of orange trees lining the way that led to our ranch-style home. I was way past my curfew and a little drunk. As we slowly drove up the long driveway, we saw my dad standing at the top of the drive holding a shotgun. Ed stopped, turned to me and said, "Just because we're late?"

It turned out that dad thought he had heard a burglar. He had grabbed his shotgun (which he had no idea how to use) and had run out to look for the would-be criminal. Ed was so elated that my dad harbored no ill will for him that he jumped out of his car to help dad find the bad guy. Meanwhile, I sneaked into the house, jumped into my adored canopy bed and feigned sleep. That was my first and last date with Ed! By the way... they never found the bad guy!

Another date that deserves to be retold also revolved around my father and his eccentricities. This was another first date that also ended badly. This time as we slowly drove up the drive to our home, we found my father outside feverishly playing his violin in the moonlight. To get the full picture of this scenario, I need to give you an explicit view of my father.

It was a warm, sultry August night. My dad was wearing shorty PJs and an open cotton bathrobe. My dad was pretty much bald and my mother would often crochet him skullcaps to keep his head warm. These looked a lot like a Yamaka! He wore one that night, and coupled with my dad's prominent nose, he could have passed for *The Fiddler on the Roof*.

Dad had also dragged his music stand into the front yard and jerry-rigged a flashlight to shine on his music. He swayed as he played his violin. For some reason, he favored the outdoor acoustics and thought his playing was superb outside on a starlit night! Of course, my date was shocked. My date slowed down enough for me to get out of the car and then flew out the driveway. It was yet another solitary date!

I certainly enjoyed those fleeting, skinny days. I wore many new clothes in single-digit sizes. At the university, I was the Queen of the Wednesday Night Stomp (a study break) where I feverishly danced and gyrated; I even smoked! However, I never learned how to inhale... worst-case scenario... lip cancer!

I was at my skinniest when I spent an academic semester abroad. I was housed in Salzburg,

Austria, with thirty fellow students from the U of Redlands. We were housed and took all course work (Humanities and German) in Salzburg. Periodically, we would board a luxury bus liner and head to a new country to explore. During that semester we visited, France, England, Germany, Scotland, Ireland, Wales, Italy, Luxemburg, and Czechoslovakia, along with the amazing countryside.

It was an awesome experience that I will never forget. For the first few months, I had no trouble keeping my weight in control. The girls often shared their meals with the male students who were slowly starving. Portions of meat and protein were not too plentiful.

As spring arrived, my roommate and I strolled the streets of Salzburg daily. We soon found a favorite *Konditerei* (an Austrian confectionary shop). We stopped there each day and the wonderful shop owner would stuff a bag full of delectable, free treats that we shared with fellow coeds back at the hotel. Between the pastries, beer, wine and Wienerschnitzel, some pounds slowly began to reappear, despite our long walks!

My mom had bought me some great clothes for my semester abroad. We were confined to only two suitcases for the entire semester and one of the suitcases had to be empty when we left so we could fill it up as we traveled throughout Europe.

Pantyhose and tights had recently been invented (1959), plus I always had tights and knee socks to augment my wardrobe. This served me well because I had shapely legs. As we traveled, we wore an outfit all day long; we'd add a broach or necklace and earrings for dinner, thus creating a "stylish, new look!" It got to where we only recognized each other by what we wore. At one point, I actually broke down and bought a new dress. When I wore it for the first time, nobody in our group even recognized me!

Our semester abroad ended in late June and then I traveled through Scotland, Ireland, and Wales that summer with one of my fellow students. He and I were on tight budgets. In those days, one could travel on about $1 per day for lodging and scant meals. By the time I reached home, I had redropped all the additional pounds, and then some! I looked fantastic in a pair of Lederhosen!

Following my semester abroad, where I had unfettered freedom, it was nearly impossible to move back in with my parents for the rest of that summer. They were delighted to have me home and damn near smothered me with love!

The fall of my senior year, I started to readjust to life on a college campus. Of course it was wonderful to reunite with all my college buddies, and we spent many evenings at the local *Gay Nineties Pizza Parlor* throwing down beers and slices! Still, my head and heart remained in Salzburg and I was often melancholy.

And, as all formerly chubby girls know, this became the perfect storm for regaining weight! By the time graduation rolled around, I was 15 pounds heavier, still looking good, but destined to further blossom out! Thank God my graduation robe concealed my weight gain!

I needed a 5th year of post-graduate work to obtain my California Teaching Credential. I chose UCI for my 5TH year course work. I lived on Balboa Island with two of my former UR buddies. That was a tumultuous year and my waistline showed it! Student Teaching was very intimidating! I taught German II and German IV at Newport Harbor High and German I at a local, intermediate school.

Since I was a young, obviously an inexperienced teacher, I often faced daily challenges. I had great German skills, but dealing with obstinate teenagers was a daunting challenge! I had never thought that any student would think less of me because I was only a few years older than they were.

Thankfully, I had a wonderful Master Teacher who taught me the necessary managerial skills I needed to deal with rowdy teenagers. I passed all my student teaching courses and received a lifetime teaching credential for California. Sadly, one of my fondest memories of that period of my life was the great food they served at Newport Harbor High. They offered a daily breakfast for teachers provided by a student culinary class. The food was yummy and cheap. I ate breakfast there daily as I watched my waistline expand.

During my student teaching days, I maintained a part-time job as a waitress in a Mexican restaurant in Newport Beach. There I discovered my addiction for Mexican food and a fondness of making money. Nightly, I would race home to count my tips. I actually made more money working as a part-time waitress than I made in my first three years as a teacher!

Actually, I had never planned to teach. I wanted to be Doris Day. The main reason my parents pushed me into education was that they thought that teaching was a noble profession and that my sister had pursued teaching. In those days there were few opportunities for careers for women: Teacher

– Nurse – Librarian – Secretary - Stewardess. However, reality bit me. My parents had paid for five years of college. It was now my turn to step up to the plate! They were no longer going to support me!

At UCI there was a board filled with career opportunities. I found a high school looking for a German/English teacher. On a lark and armed with a donut for the drive, I headed towards LA for my first interview. It was a relatively new high school, directly across the street from a *Granny Goose* factory and adjacent to the train tracks. It was not located in the best part of town.

My interview, by today's standards, was intrusive. However, in the early 70s, I was fair game. Most questions revolved around my personal life, not on my teaching abilities. I knew there were candidates with far more German teaching experience than I, but I soon realized, I would be the cheapest candidate for hire. I accepted the position and after I left that infamous interview, I headed directly to a *Del Taco* for some celebratory tacos! Let my weight gain continue!

During that first year of teaching, I managed to survive with the help from food and my husband. By year's end I had gained another 30 pounds, but my husband still loved me! As the years flew by, my weight remained in a constant state of flux. At my heaviest, I topped the scales at around 280 pounds. Today, I hover around 170 pounds. I will never be skinny, but I'm content with my current weight and, yes, my husband still loves me!

I was only at a "normal' weight for a few glorious years, but in my head, I remained fat. I can remember a dear friend from college telling me, "Don't walk like a fat lady, you're not fat anymore!" Indeed, the ".05% Factor" remains the one weight goal I achieved! However, I have truly enjoyed the other 99.95% of my life! Time for some Rocky Road ice cream!

The Chubby Girl's Abbreviated Guide for Fashion and Dieting
Chapter 11

You decide!

Fashion / Diet	True	Myth
Every body style can wear stripes.		
Calories really don't matter.		
Donuts are much healthier than beans.		
Creamy salad dressings have fewer calories.		
Wear dark colors and look fifty pounds lighter.		
Large girls should always wear white, 3" thick patent leather belts.		
Avoid drinking too much water.		
If possible, avoid unnecessary calories and skip breakfast.		
When possible, avoid eating cottage cheese.		

A List of Synonyms for the Word "Chubby"
Chapter 12

As we mature, we often outgrow the word "chubby" and need to find a new term to describe our more mature appearance. Hopefully, it's a kind reflection that shuns how we secretly feel about our body image. However, sometimes it ends up being the kind of descriptive term that shatters our confidence and makes one want to eat everything in sight! Here are some new options to consider, in no particular order:

TUBBY

PLUMP

ROLY-POLY

ROUND

PORTLY

STOUT

DUMPY

CHUNKY

BROAD IN THE BEAM

WELL PADDED

AMPLE

BIG

BUTTERBALL

BUXOM

FULL-FIGURED

HEFTY

HUSKY

ROTUND

WELL UPHOLSTERED

ZAFTIG

PLEASINGLY PLUMP

FAT

Have you found a word that works for you?

Acknowledgments

These folks encouraged me and supported me as I wrote these stories. They were my cheerleaders.
- Bill Jerome - my husband for 49 years and counting
- Mrs. Kary Bemoll – my former colleague and friend
- Mrs. Sue Fassett – my niece and lover of books
- Mrs. Chris McCrystal – my friend for the past 50 years
- Mrs. Marilyn McDowell – my former colleague and friend
- Mrs. Katie Mullaly – Publisher & Owner of Surrogate Press
- Mr. Mark Nelson – my personal trainer and friend

About the Author

Jean M. Jerome was an avid tennis player for over 30 years and attended countless tennis tournaments as a spectator. She was unable to show the same prowess for golf, however she played bad golf for many years. Her other loves include listening to music and reading. But, writing is her favorite avocation.

She spent 38 years in the education system. Throughout that time, she taught English and German, was Director of Activities and Special Projects coordinator, and was an A.P. Curriculum Administrator, among many other responsibilities. She received special awards during her tenure, including a yearbook dedication that she still treasures today.

www.ingramcontent.com/pod-product-compliance
Lightning Source LLC
Chambersburg PA
CBHW030156100526
44592CB00009B/302